Dear Parents,

Welcome to the Scholastic Reader serie years of experience with teachers, paren into a program that is designed to matcl and skills.

Level 1— Short sentences and stories n⸱ ⸱⸱ up of words kids can sound out using their phonics skills and words that are important to remember.

Level 2— Longer sentences and stories with words kids need to know and new "big" words that they will want to know.

Level 3— From sentences to paragraphs to longer stories, these books have large "chunks" of texts and are made up of a rich vocabulary.

Level 4— First chapter books with more words and fewer pictures.

It is important that children learn to read well enough to succeed in school and beyond. Here are ideas for reading this book with your child:

- Look at the book together. Encourage your child to read the title and make a prediction about the story.
- Read the book together. Encourage your child to sound out words when appropriate. When your child struggles, you can help by providing the word.
- Encourage your child to retell the story. This is a great way to check for comprehension.
- Have your child take the fluency test on the last page to check progress.

Scholastic Readers are designed to support your child's efforts to learn how to read at every age and every stage. Enjoy helping your child learn to read and love to read.

　　　　—Francie Alexander
　　　　　Chief Education Officer
　　　　　Scholastic Education

For my brother Robert – who's always going somewhere
—M.B.P.
For Elliot, Avery, and Adelan
—B.K.

ISBN 0-439-59891-5

Text copyright © 2005 by Marjorie Blain Parker.
Illustrations copyright © 2005 by Bob Kolar.
All rights reserved. Published by Scholastic Inc.
SCHOLASTIC, CARTWHEEL BOOKS, and associated logos
are trademarks and/or registered trademarks of Scholastic Inc.

Library of Congress Cataloging-in-Publication Data is available.

10 9 8 7 6 5 4 3 2   06 07 08
Printed in the U.S.A. 23 • First printing, February 2005

Hello, Freight Train!

by **Marjorie Blain Parker**

Illustrated by **Bob Kolar**

Scholastic Reader — Level 1

SCHOLASTIC INC.

Cartwheel BOOKS ®

New York Toronto London Auckland Sydney
Mexico City New Delhi Hong Kong Buenos Aires

Lights flash and bells ring.
Down, down goes the gate.

**Here comes the freight train.
We watch as we wait.**

The engine is first,
so bold and so strong.

It pulls all the cars that follow along.

Hello, freight train!

Here comes a flat car, a hopper, a rack car.

Here comes a boxcar,
and a big piggyback car . . .

**cars with chickens,
cows, and hogs,**

cars with lumber,
coal, and logs.

Tank cars for gas.
Tank cars for oil.

Refrigerator cars
where food won't spoil.

The train rolls away,
far down the track.

The last car's light blinks from the back.

Good-bye, freight train!

Fluency Fun

The words in each list below end in the same sounds.
Read the words in a list.
Read them again.
Read them faster.
Try to read all 12 words in one minute.

back	**bar**	**pain**
black	**car**	**rain**
rack	**far**	**brain**
track	**star**	**train**

Look for these words in the story.

down		**here**
for	**comes**	**with**

Note to Parents:

According to *A Dictionary of Reading and Related Terms,* fluency is "the ability to read smoothly, easily, and readily with freedom from word-recognition problems." Fluency is necessary for good comprehension and enjoyable reading. The activities on this page include a speed drill and a sight-recognition drill. Speed drills build fluency because they help students rapidly recognize common syllables and spelling patterns in words, and they're fun! Sight-recognition drills help students smoothly and accurately recognize words. Practice these activities with your child to help him or her become a fluent reader.

—**Wiley Blevins,**
Reading Specialist